WEIDER WEIGHT TRAINING FOR WOMEN

BETTER *Body* BETTER *Shape*

WEIDER WEIGHT TRAINING FOR WOMEN

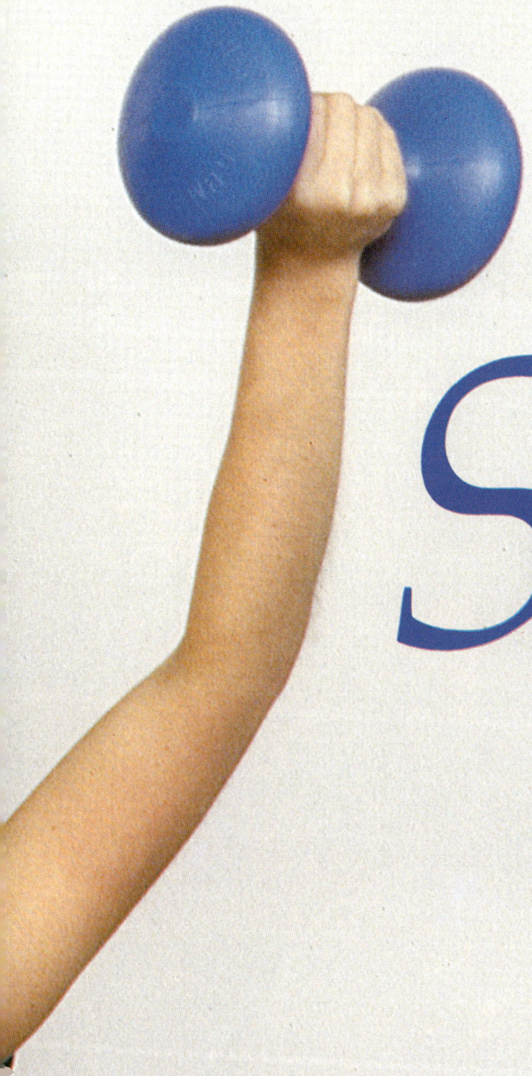

Better Body Better Shape

JOANNE DAY

HAMLYN

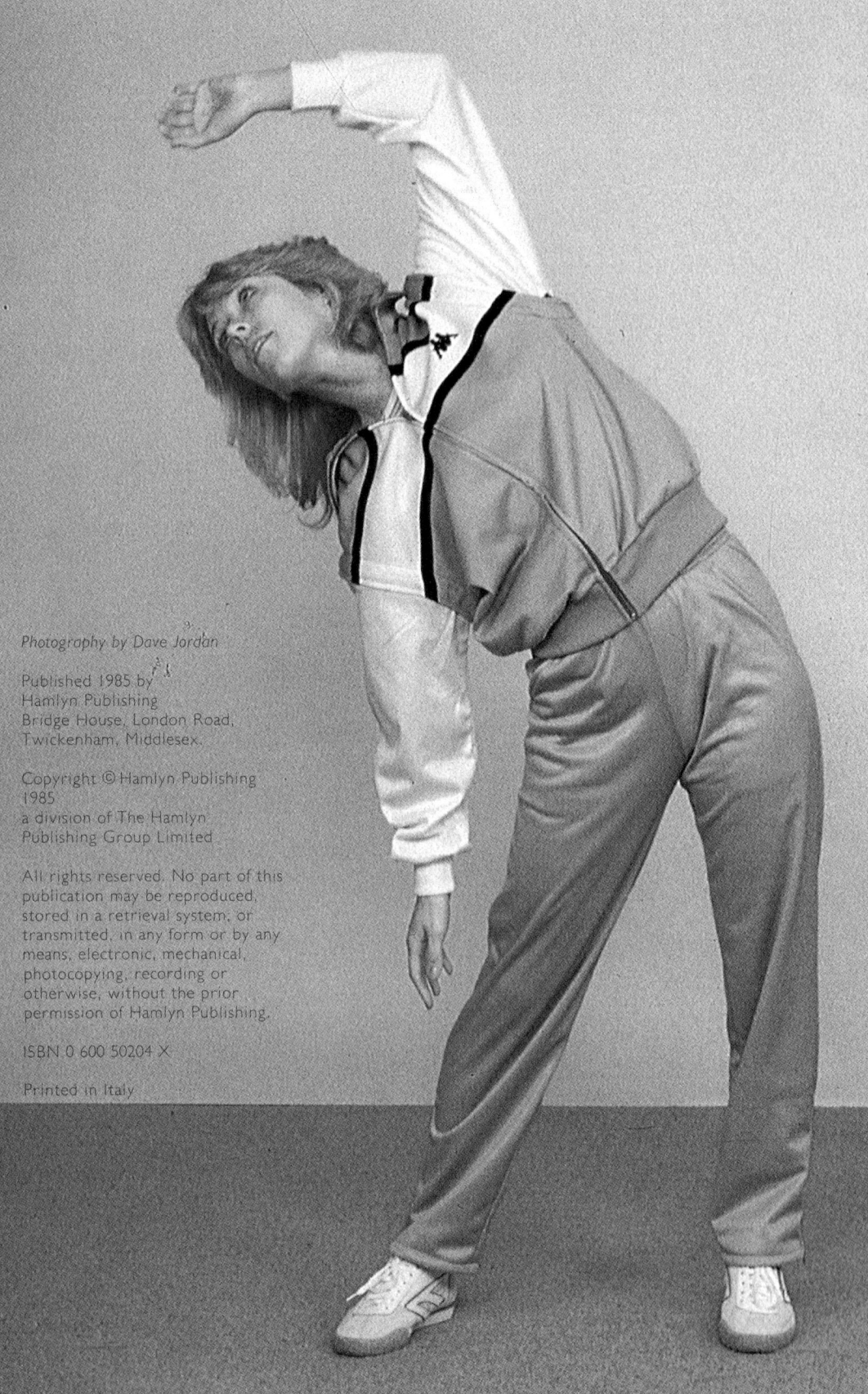

Photography by Dave Jordan

Published 1985 by
Hamlyn Publishing
Bridge House, London Road,
Twickenham, Middlesex.

Copyright © Hamlyn Publishing
1985
a division of The Hamlyn
Publishing Group Limited

All rights reserved. No part of this
publication may be reproduced,
stored in a retrieval system, or
transmitted, in any form or by any
means, electronic, mechanical,
photocopying, recording or
otherwise, without the prior
permission of Hamlyn Publishing.

ISBN 0 600 50204 X

Printed in Italy

Contents

Introduction 10
Getting Started 14
Warming-up Exercises 18
Safety in the Gym 28
Weight-Training Exercises 31
Equipping a Home Gym 54
Diet and Vitamins 58
Maintaining Enthusiasm 60

Introduction

Very few women are satisfied or unconcerned with their bodies, either from a practical, physical point of view, or from that of an attractive appearance. Most are influenced by photographs of models in glossy magazines, with long, slim legs and tiny waists. Somehow success and happiness seem to go hand in hand with those beautiful figures. Success is important to everyone. I have enjoyed many successes since I became interested in weight-training and fitness. Reaching a goal in regard to bodyshaping is a relatively easy success. Weight-training is effective and fun.

Although there are ways of disguising a "problem area" of the body by clever use of clothes and accessories, women remain aware of the parts of their bodies they would like to change. Many women complain of having "big legs" or "flabby tummy" and it really does seem to be a problem for them. I had the good fortune of having my weaknesses bluntly pointed out to me about four years ago. I say "good fortune", because it gave me the impetus to do something about them. Since then, training with weights is proving to be a most effective and enjoyable way of giving me the shape I want, and as I am made of the same material as everyone else, I see no reason why others should not benefit by following a training programme to suit their needs.

The full benefits of fitness and bodyshaping I discovered as I progressed, and some are more important to me now than those I aimed at when I started.

Fit for anything
With a slim, firmer body you will find that your body does more than just cope, it excels at the problems you continually set it, from everyday jobs such as carrying shopping and taking children to school, to more physical activities like running for buses or digging the garden. Bodies have been expertly designed to work, and not just to be pampered. If treated properly, like a car they function better.

Once you start to get fitter you will be amazed at the feeling of exhilaration you get from coping with physical problems that would previously have been a burden, particularly if normally you lead a sedentary life. In addition to coping with usual activities you will have energy and strength to tackle new ones—perhaps walking or swimming. I have found a kind of circle exists—if my weight-training goes well, I have enthusiasm to attempt new things which in turn leads to additional keenness to carry on with the weight-training. Success is infectious.

Shaping your body is only a small part of being "fit", which again is just a sub-section of "health", but one good thing leads to another, and many find their better body inspires them to adopt a healthier diet through choice—not because someone told them it was a good idea. And that leads to more enthusiasm for a better body shape—it is the circle effect again.

Relaxation
Another important aspect of my life which has improved since I started weight-training is my ability to relax. A hard day's work will make anyone tired but frequently people complain that although they feel tired and worn out, they are unable to relax. Concentrating on a weight-training exercise shuts out the rest of the world and makes it impossible to worry about everyday anxieties. Many people say that since improving their fitness and health they have been able to sleep better and wake next morning feeling refreshed and full of vitality.

Mental attitude

Today's woman is looking for satisfaction, independence and self-esteem in her life, so modern magazines tell us. Many people say that since starting a training programme they have felt good mentally. There is something about setting a target and working for it that boosts self-esteem. With weight-training, although there are people willing to help and guide you, only you can decide just how much effort you are going to put in. Being able to work and push your limits gradually higher, will give you, too, confidence and belief in yourself.

Bodyshaping

For most people the reason for commencing a training programme is to reshape the body. Weight-training is proving to be a most effective way of doing this.

The main doubt most women have about weight-training is the fear they will look muscular and masculine. This is a misapprehension. Women have a different hormone structure from men which prevents this happening naturally. I know several girls who compete in physical culture competitions who train exceedingly hard for years and stick rigidly to a diet, putting in far more effort than would a woman wanting just to improve her shape, and they look far from masculine—quite the reverse. They use weights to enhance a feminine body and to create shapely legs, firm tummy and good shaped upper body. Remember: being soft and round does not necessarily make a body feminine—many men have these qualities.

The traditional "hour-glass" image of a feminine body requires a V-shaped top half and a smaller, tight mid-section. These do not always come naturally—they have to be worked at.

Success for everyone
One of the main reasons weight-training can be successful for everyone is that it can be specific and individual. A whole class of people does not have exactly the same needs and so does not need exactly the same programme. A programme can be individually tailored.

The majority of women wanting to improve their shape want to do so by losing weight. Dieting, while making a person lose weight, is not going to leave them with a firm, well-shaped body. At the same time it would be false to say weight-training alone is going to make a person lose weight. Obviously, weight-training exercises use energy and therefore calories. The activity has the effect of increasing the rate of metabolism and recent research has shown that calories are burned up quicker for up to 24 hours after the exercise. Demand for oxygen during exercise can be increased by ten times as the body needs energy, using stored fat in the process. Energy to supply the effort comes from the food eaten and fat stored, often conspicuously, around the body. So if your diet is controlled and you work the muscle harder, you begin to use the surrounding fat to supply energy.

Monitoring progress
Enthusiasm is maintained if you can see the results of the effort you are putting into an activity. Have a photograph of yourself in a "before" stage so that it can be compared with "after". Monitoring weight on scales is not adequate because the weight might be fat or muscle. Even if your shape is changing dramatically it does not necessarily mean there will be a huge weight-loss. Progress is monitored by appearance and the way you feel.

Remember to set yourself a goal so that there is something to work towards. Remember also that the time taken to reach a goal is going to depend on the amount of work put in. Training two or three times a week is adequate to improve the shape to an acceptable standard but not, perhaps, to win a Miss Universe. However, the most important thing is to enjoy it so you do it as often or as seldom as you want.

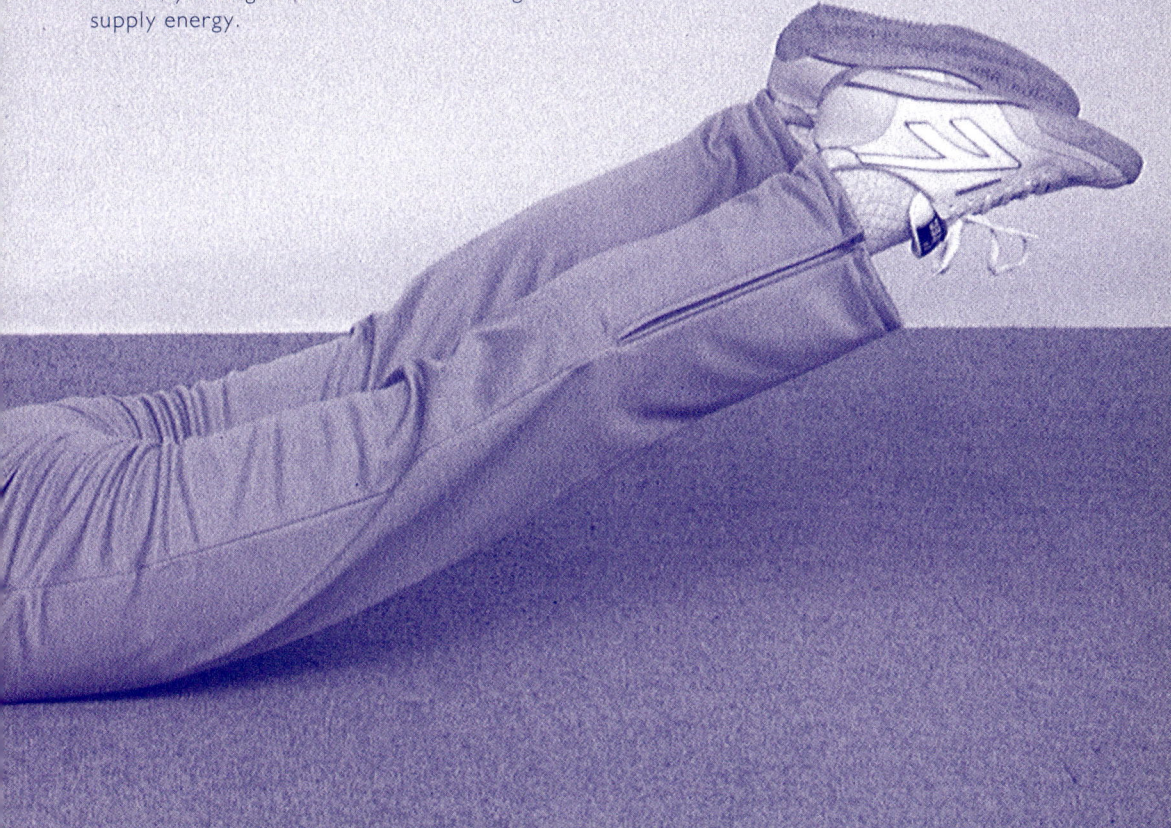

Getting Started

When you have decided that weight-training can do something for you, the next stage is to find somewhere to put this enthusiasm into practice. Now that training and sports activities are fashionable, that is much easier to do than it was a few years ago, when weight-training women were considered to be somewhat weird! Most towns now have at least one weight-training gym and many leisure and sports centres have facilities. These facilities range from adequate but basic equipment to plush "health clubs" which provide additional leisure facilities such as jacuzzi, sunbeds, even bars. There is of course a corresponding price range. You should be able to find somewhere to suit your needs; but do remember you are going, primarily, to work out and not pamper yourself. Effective ways of finding a gym are to ask in a sports shop, and to look for advertisements in the local newspapers.

Choosing a gym
The most important factor when choosing a place to train is the staff who work there. They will be the ones giving you help and tuition to ensure that you get maximum benefit from your effort while avoiding the risk of injury. I was privileged to train from the beginning at Jim's Gym, where Christine Charles epitomizes what you should look for: an instructor interested and keen on the sport, who is willing to give individual attention, and lead by example. It is often a good indication to look at the instructor's body to decide for yourself if you can have any faith in what she tells you.

Rows of shiny weights and complicated machinery can look impressive or intimidating depending on your frame of mind, but it is important to ensure that your particular standard is catered for. For example, you do not want to pay out a lot of money to discover later that the gym is designed for power weight lifters. Remember that you will, initially, progress rapidly and so you are shortly going to need more than a small, limited amount of equipment.

Even though you are going to spend only $1\frac{1}{2}$ to 2 hours in the gym, check the opening hours before you join. You do not want to find it closed when you most want to use it.

Many people prefer to train with a partner rather than alone. Apart from the practical advantages of having someone to help out there is much to be gained from having the encouragement and support of someone else.

Personally, I enjoy the club atmosphere of training in a gym, and do not think a beginner need feel intimidated about joining a club; most people are willing to help. You will not be a beginner for long—you will be surprised at how quickly you progress.

If there are any physical or medical factors which concern you about the advisability of your starting training, or indeed any exercise, then do get a medical opinion first from your doctor.

Clothing
So long as you are sensible it is easy to enjoy the sport without having to spend a lot of money on fancy gym wear.

The main feature, obviously, is comfort—ensure that you are not buying something with a seam so placed to rub and make your skin sore midway through the work-out. Although I do not favour very loose clothing that flaps around, it is important that the design is not restrictive when you move. Look at the fabric used—obviously cotton is cooler. You must also consider that your clothes are going to be washed a lot.

Jogging and tracksuits are very popular; they are functional in keeping you warm, designed for their purpose, and are now fashionable.

Buy suitable shoes that are going to protect your feet (like those I am wearing in the photographs). Never train in socks or bare feet—you risk hurting yourself.

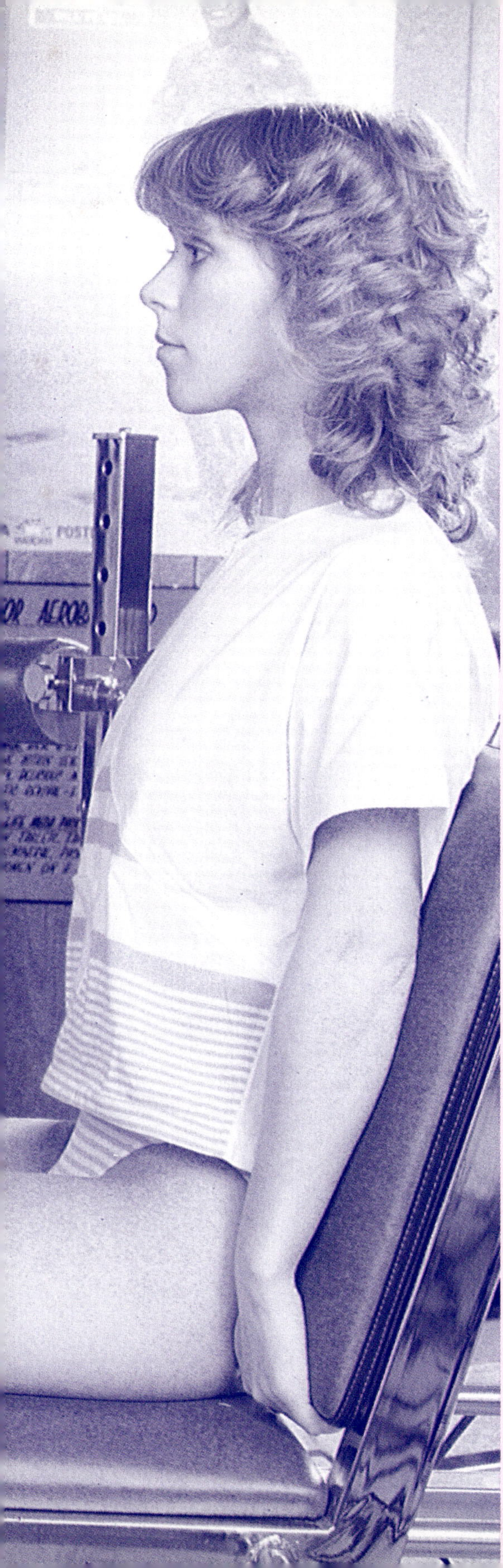

If you cannot have a shower and change clothes at the gym then ensure that you have something extra to put on prior to going outside. You will have got very warm inside the gym and should avoid getting cold straight away.

Do not train wearing jewellery; apart from the fact that it is unnecessary, it is also dangerous. Chains and rings could get caught with disastrous results.

Warming-up Exercises

Warming up is important for getting the body and mind ready for exercise. There may be times when you do not feel able to cope with a full weights session and you may only want to do the warming-up session.

You will not benefit from trying to train if your heart is not in it. Listen to what your body tells you. If you have an ache or pain it is better to miss a session. Training is fun not a burden.

If you are not very active and fit I would suggest that you do the warm-up session only for two or three weeks—maybe more if you are not particularly young—before attempting to use weights. Do not try to do all the exercises the first week, and do each exercise only once to begin with. Eventually, each exercise will be performed with comfort, and you can begin repeating them in a session.

A warm-up session serves to mobilize the joints, stretch muscles and gradually increase the work being done by the heart and lungs. The session should last at least five minutes and preferably 15 minutes.

Exercises to loosen joints should be performed fairly briskly with free movement. Do not try to force a limb into a position that feels unnatural or painful. So long as you are working as hard as you can it does not matter if your neighbour seems to be doing better. The benefits will be the same. The exercises are designed to start at the top with the neck and shoulders and to work downwards so that all parts of the body are involved.

Neck and Shoulder Exercises

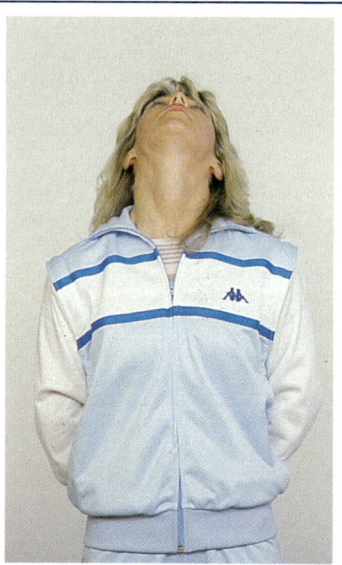

a

a Circle head round, ten times.

b Shrug shoulders in a circular fashion, ten times.

c Arm swings: Make circles with arms ten times, then perform free swings forward and backward ten times. Do both arms together. Arms do not have to be locked straight.

Trunk Bending and Twists

a Bent-over waist twists: stand with feet slightly wider than shoulder width apart, and bend over with shoulders level with hips. Twist the upper body so that with both arms straight you touch the right ankle with the left hand and then alternate. Do not raise the shoulders up and down—just twist the mid-section.

To begin with you may feel easier having the knees slightly flexed. You can do this for as long as you want, breathing in and out with alternate swings.

b *Side bends: from a straight standing position bend sideways, not forwards, so that the right hand runs down the right leg, while the left arm bends up and over the head. It is not as awful as it sounds—just bend as far as you can without leaning forward. Repeat with the other arm and leg. Breathe out as you go down, in as you come up.*

Do each side ten times.

c *Touch toes: stand with feet slightly wider than shoulder width, standing upright, with shoulders back (it is important with any exercise that you develop good posture—think of the strict style rather than cheating as you only cheat yourself).*

Bend forward to touch the toes, breathing out as you go down. Keep the legs straight—do not bend them just so that you get closer to your toes. You will soon progress. Do ten bends.

b

c

Hips and Legs Exercises

a Leg swings: standing upright with something to hold for support, swing one leg forwards and back. Do 20 swings on each leg. Then turn around and swing one leg out to the side, then back across your body. Do 20 swings on each leg. Try to concentrate on mobilizing the hips and not just trying to get your leg as high as possible by bending your back.

b Lunges: stand with back straight, one leg stretched in front, the other behind. Bend both knees so that the back knee touches the floor, then push yourself back up so that both legs are straight. Try to ensure that you do not have the legs too close together. This is one reason for overbalancing—another is leaning too far forward with the head bent down. Breathe in going down, and out coming up. Do ten lunges on each leg.

You should be able to feel this exercise working the hips, top and inside of the leg.

c Kick backs: start by kneeling on all fours. The left knee is bent up to the chin, bringing the head down towards it, then kick it back and upward, straightening the leg and pushing the head back. Breathe out when the leg is bent in and in as you push it back. Do ten kick backs on each leg.

This exercise is working the hips and bottom.

c

d Knee bends (squats): stand upright with the feet shoulder width apart and the back straight and keep it like that throughout the exercise. Bend the knees down as far as you can without bending your back, then push back up straight. Do ten squats. Breathe in going down, out coming up.

e Side lunges: stand with legs stretched wide apart. Bend one knee while the other stretches out to the side. You will feel this pull on the inside of the thigh. Do not try to make it pull too much, just go down as far as you comfortably can. Repeat with the other knee. Hold each down position for a count of four — it is the stretch position that is important here, not doing the exercise quickly. Do ten lunges on each leg.

f Hamstring exercise (stretching the muscle at the back of the leg): stand with legs astride, arms out to the side. Lean forward from the hips so that the body is parallel to the floor.

Slightly bounce the body so that you can feel a pull on the back of the leg. Do ten bounces.

If you really want, you can make this harder by bending further so that the hands touch the floor and then walk them backwards and forwards!

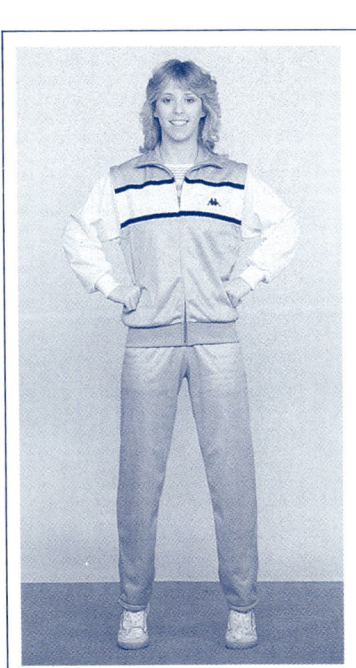

g Calf raises: stand with the feet shoulder width apart. Raise yourself up on to the toes and lower, not drop, yourself back on to the heels. Do it with the feet pointing in front, then pointing inwards, then pointing outwards. Do 20 calf raises each way.

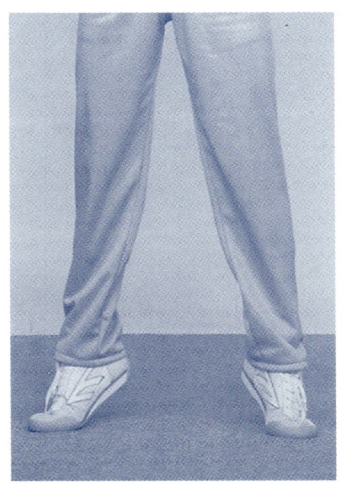
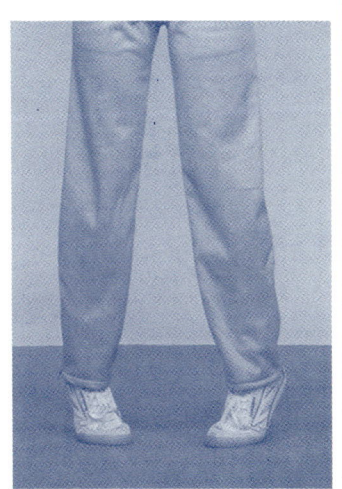

Back Exercises

These exercises are incorporated to help to strengthen the back in preparation for weight-training. They also have the additional benefit of helping to firm the buttocks.

Start by lying flat on your front. Lift the left leg up, keeping it straight, and count to ten. Then slowly lower. Repeat with the other leg. Do three on each leg. Then raise both feet together, and count to ten (it is cheating to count in twos). Do three times. Next stretch your arms in front and raise both arms and legs at the same time, and count to ten. Do three times.

I do my abdominal exercises (see page 46) at this point as a way of warming up. If you do the same thing ensure that you are warm and have loosened up the joints before you head for the weights.

Although I have suggested the number of times to do each exercise, do fewer if you feel uncomfortable, especially for the first few sessions. Gradually increase the number as you feel able. The exercises I have suggested are by no means comprehensive or exhaustive, as I see them solely as a preliminary to the real session—with weights. They prepare for training and maintain suppleness.

Safety in the Gym

The gym is, potentially, a very dangerous place, but with care and thought need cause no concern. A couple of safety factors were mentioned in the section on clothing. The next consideration is with the weights.

If you are training with the type of bar to which you add your own selection of weights, be sure to use collars on the end of the bar. Without these collars fitted, if you accidentally tip to one side there could be foot-shattering results.

Before starting an exercise consider the space around you with regard to other people and equipment. You need to be aware of the movement your neighbour is making so that you can avoid a collision in the middle. With so many mirrors around there could be a lot of bad luck!

One of the most dangerous things you can do is to leave discarded weights and equipment lying on the floor. This is my particular pet hate as it was the cause of the only injury I have suffered in training. You can quite easily return equipment to its place during the time between exercises.

Possibly even more dangerous than leaving equipment on the floor is to leave dumbells and small bars lying across benches. With so many people moving around carrying weights they can very easily be knocked off and cause injuries.

If you are training using machines instead of free weights then always ensure that the pin used to determine the amount of weight used is pushed in securely, as far as it will go into its hole. If it is not you might be surprised how far it can fly and how sharp it feels.

Remember to ensure always that you are "warmed-up" and have stretched adequately before starting on weights.

Remember the hint in the clothing section: never wear jewellery.

You may want to consider using a leather belt to support the lower half of the back. My advice to a beginner or to the average trainer is first of all to ensure that you are keeping a good style. Regularly do some back exercises, such as the ones in the warming-up section, and be aware of the stresses you are putting on your back both while training and when lifting weights in between exercises. Wearing a belt is not to be thought of as a substitute for keeping a good style, or insurance against not doing the exercise properly.

Weight-Training Exercises

Everyone who starts weight-training is looking for a different result. Some people want to lose weight, others to build up their bodies. The traditional "pear-shape" needs to do a bit of both. A relatively small number of popular exercises will cater for all needs. That is why they are popular—they work. The exercises in this section are for beginners, and are intended to produce an attractive overall shape if they are performed with enough effort and regularly. They are not going to make you look muscular, but you have to do some work on the muscles to improve your shape, because you cannot shape fat.

If you are a 'skinny' person, aiming to build up the body, you are advised to perform eight or ten repetitions of an exercise, and to do this three times (three sets) in a session, using as much weight as possible without cheating on the style of the exercise. After a while, when you become competent at the weight you have chosen to start on, rather than increase the number of repetitions you are doing, slightly increase the amount of weight used, so that you are still aiming to do ten repetitions.

If you are aiming to lose weight, you are advised to do at least ten to fifteen repetitions of an exercise, and again to perform three sets, but using lighter weights. Obviously this has to be combined with a weight-reducing diet and an aerobic exercise such as running or cycling.

Whatever your primary object, the exercises should be done smoothly with no jerking movements. Two or three sessions a week is sufficient for someone starting out. However, training like this means that you have to train each part of the body every time you go to the gym instead of doing one particular part of the body per session. Working in this way you will find it "easier" to do the heavier exercises, such as those for the legs and bench press exercises, first (at least it gets them over with!)

I prefer to do all of the exercises for one part of the body together before moving on to the next. Although this means that by the time of the third or fourth exercise you cannot use as much weight for the exercise as you could after a break, the muscle is being made to work hard.

When doing an exercise make the maximum use of your time and effort by considering all parts of the exercise as equally important—return slowly to the starting position, as if under resistance, and do not rush through it in relief that the exercise is over.

In order to achieve that overall, attractive, fit look it is important to do exercises for all parts of the body. Many women will be eager to do the thigh exercises but might neglect the calves, when actually the calf is the most visible part of the leg!

Leg Exercises

a Leg press: Put your feet flat against the board/bar, with the weight evenly distributed. Bend your knees in toward your chest—not too much, just enough to feel a good push from your thighs without feeling that you are working the buttocks—then push your legs back to a straight position. If, first of all, you do this exercise without weight you will find the position which is most suitable to you, that is, the one that is comfortable on your joints.

Breathe in as you bend your legs, out as you push back.

It is important to keep your back flat and straight.

I find this exercise works well on the thigh muscle without building on my hips and bottom too much.

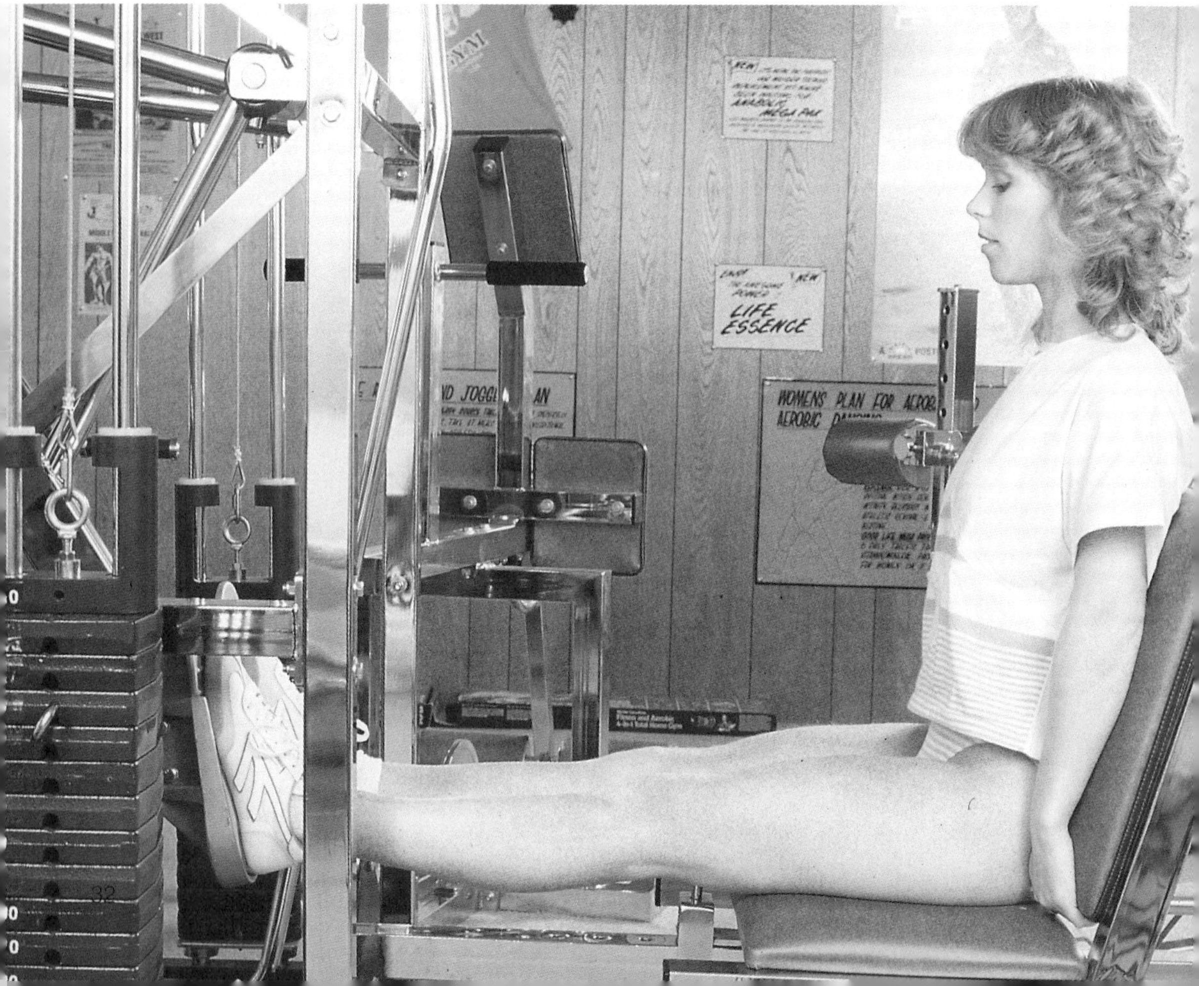

b Thigh extension. This is to firm and shape, specifically, the front of the thigh. In one, smooth movement, bring your legs up to a straight position, hold for a second and then slowly lower down again.

Breathe in as you bring your legs up, out as they go down.

A common mistake is to swing the body backwards, lifting the knees and hips off the bench. This is bad and dangerous, and will predispose to injury. Keep your back straight.

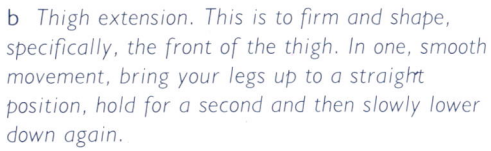

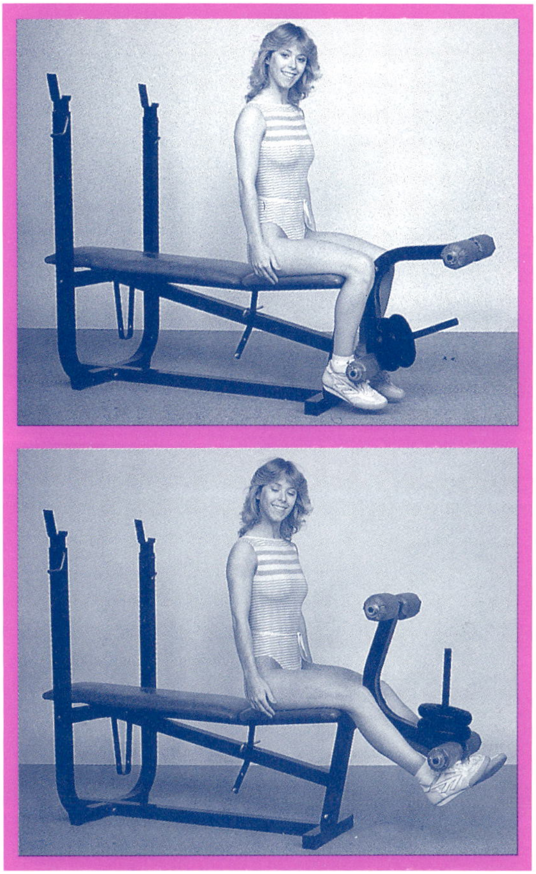

b

c Leg curls. These are usually done on the same machine as the previous exercise. They are to firm and give a rounded shape to the back of the leg, rather than the flat, dimpled appearance untrained legs sometimes have. Start off with the legs straight, then bend both knees so that your feet come up towards your back, and then, slowly, lower back down. Although I am told that this should be done without lifting the hips up off the bench I have to admit that I have yet to discover how to do that.

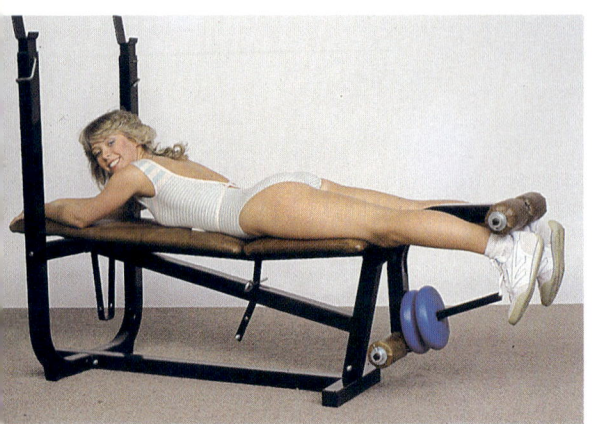

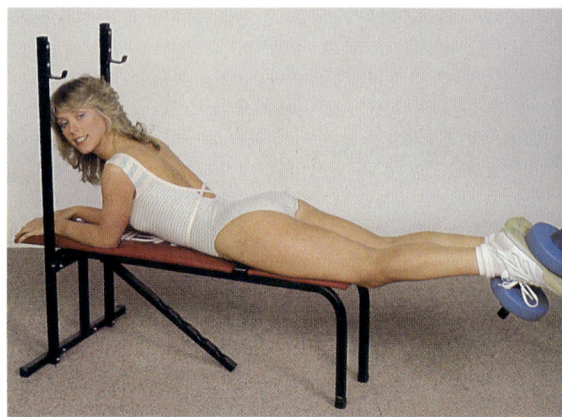

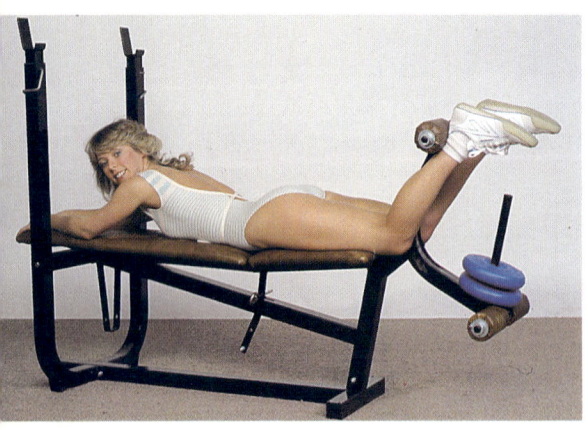

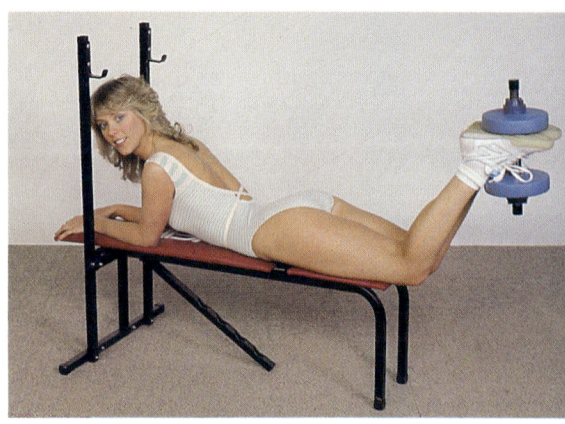

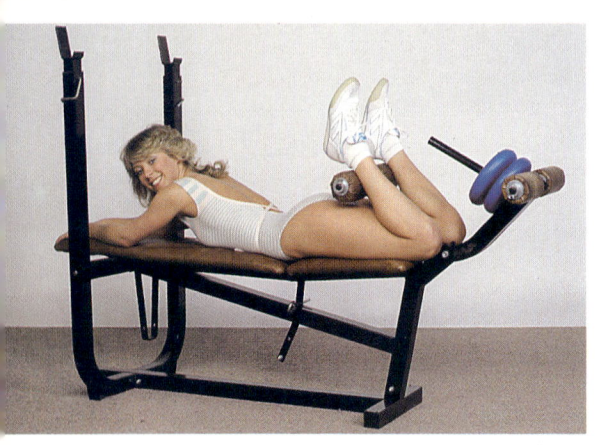

d *Lunges.* These are specifically for the inside of the thigh. If when you stand with ankles and knees together there is a little hollow above the knees or so much fat that there is an overlap, then you need to do this exercise. The procedure is as described in the warming up exercises. The bar rests across the top of the shoulders.

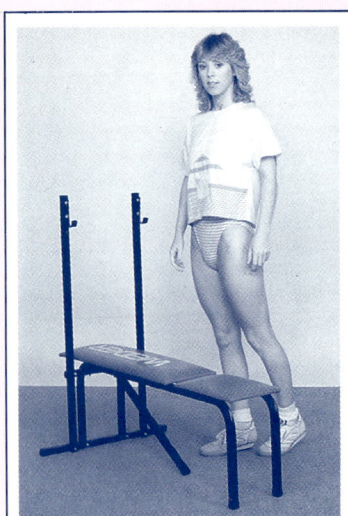

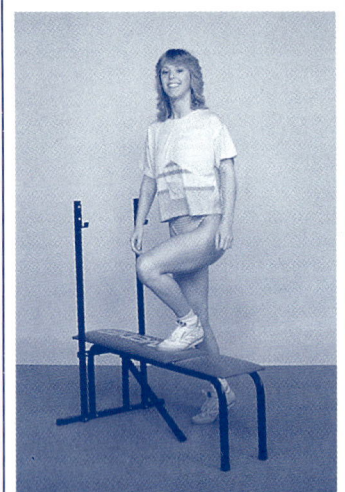

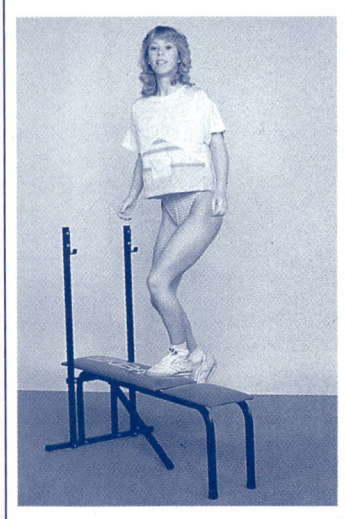

e *Step-ups.* These are for women wanting to reduce the size of their thighs. I have known step-ups to be very effective. They need to be done on something solid and stable, at least two stairs high.

Step up with the left leg first, follow with the right. The right leg is the first to go down. Swap the leading leg half-way through. Do as many as you can for as long as you can keep your back straight.

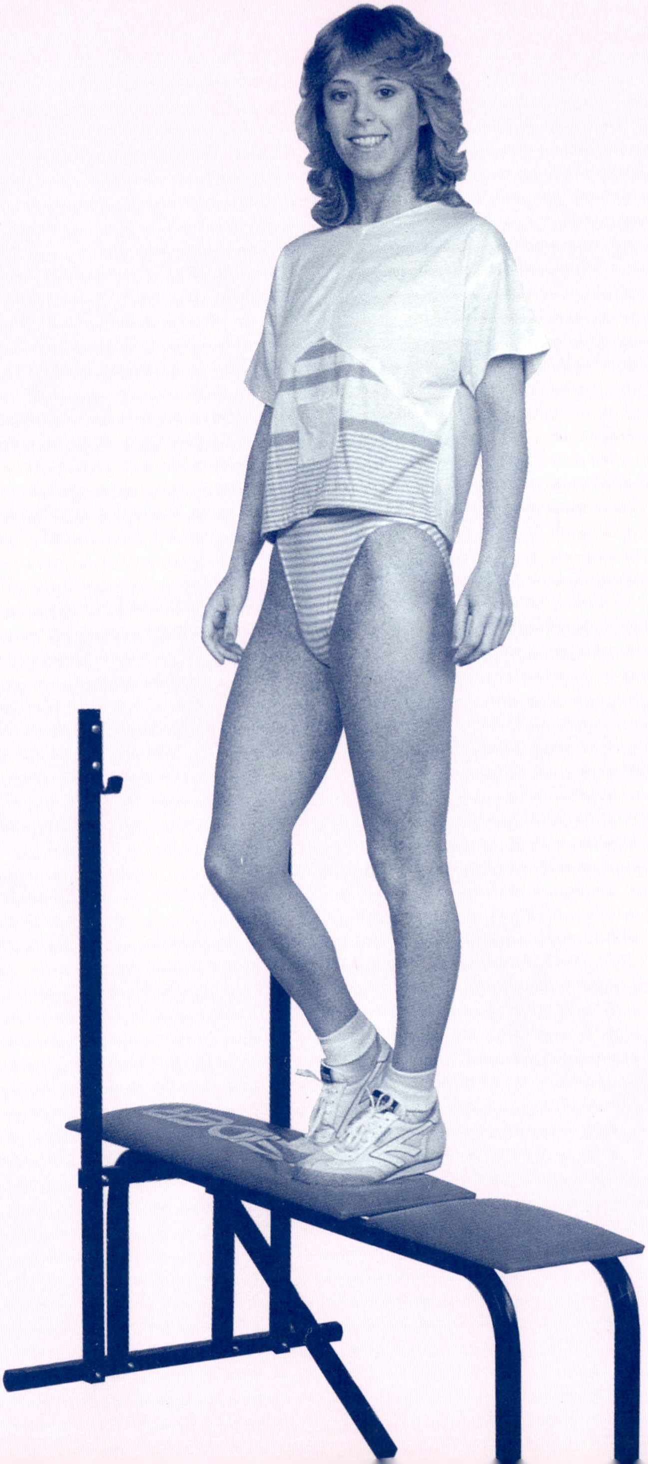

f Calf raises. These are described in the warming-up exercises. Unless you do a lot of sport you will probably find that calf raises done without weights like this will be quite adequate for a few weeks.

When you do decide to move to weights you will find the most popular machine is one where you stand with the balls of your feet on a block, and pads resting on your shoulders. The movement is done in the same way as in the warm-up.

Alternatively, you can use a leg-press machine, resting only the ball of the foot on the bar where normally the whole foot would go. Then you repeat the same movement, trying to push the weight away from you using only the ball of the foot.

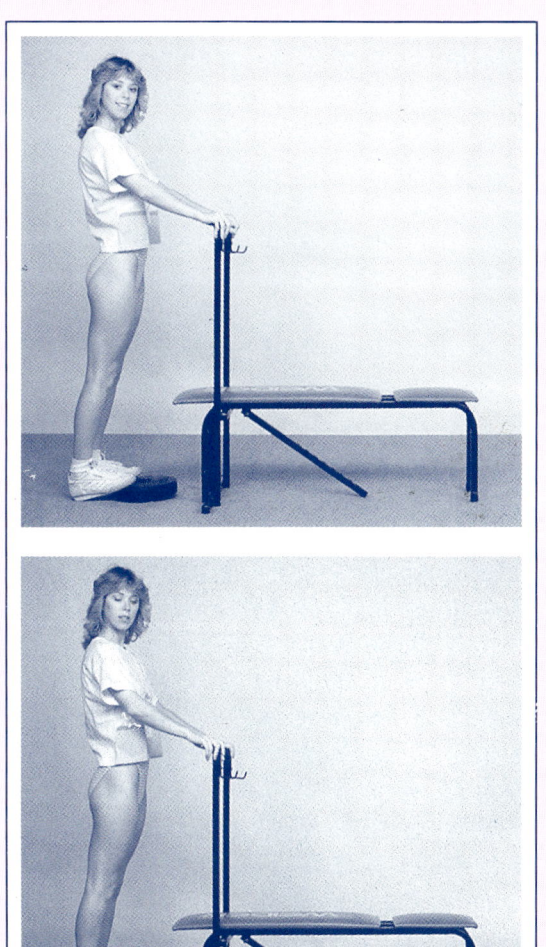

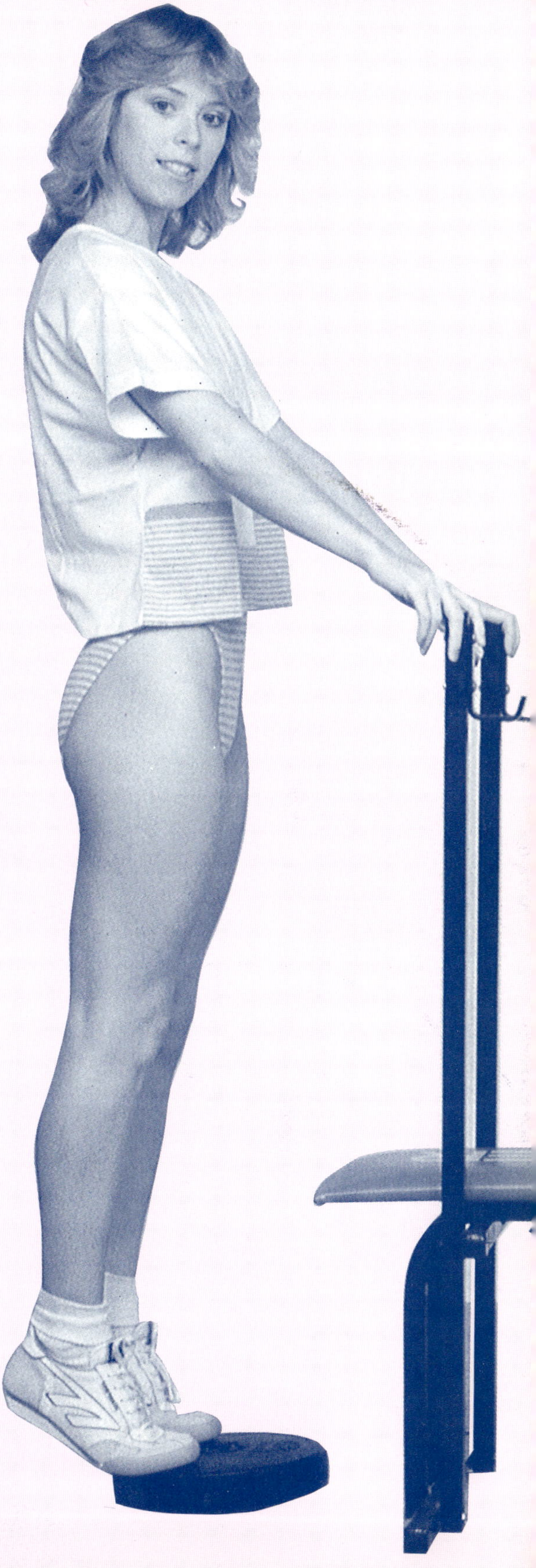

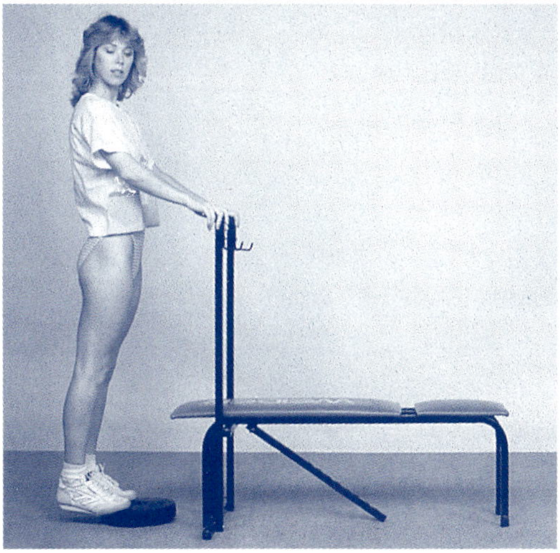

Shoulders and Chest Exercises

The next group of exercises work the shoulder and chest muscles. Trained shoulders that have a firm, rounded shape look much more attractive than scraggy bony ones; and will help a waist to look smaller, giving a 'V' shape. As for the chest exercises, well again, you cannot shape fat—the breast tissue—but these exercises will firm the surrounding and supporting muscles to improve the shape and appearance of the bust. Having toned pectoral muscles can also give the impression of a cleavage where there might not previously have been one.

a *Bench-press. Lying with your back flat on the bench, grip the bar slightly wider than shoulder width. Start with the arms stretched straight above you, bring the bar down to just above the chest, and then push it back up to the start position again.*

Breathe in coming down, out pushing back up.

It is important to keep your back flat and not to cheat by lifting your hips off the bench.

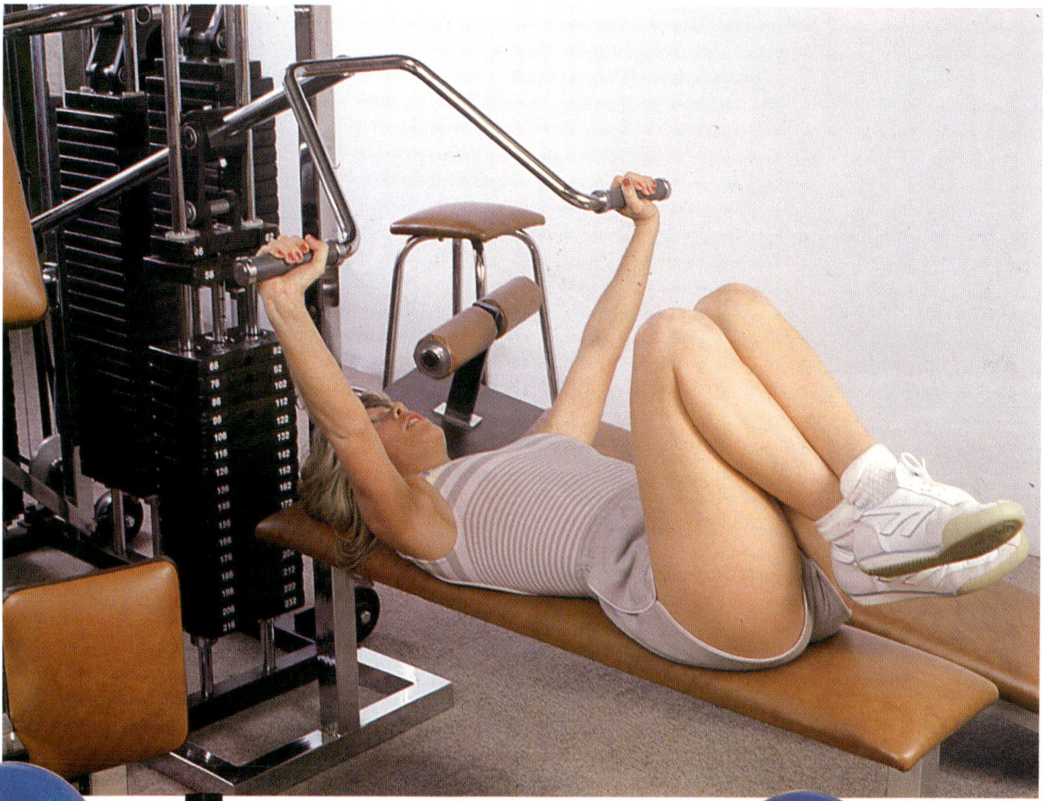

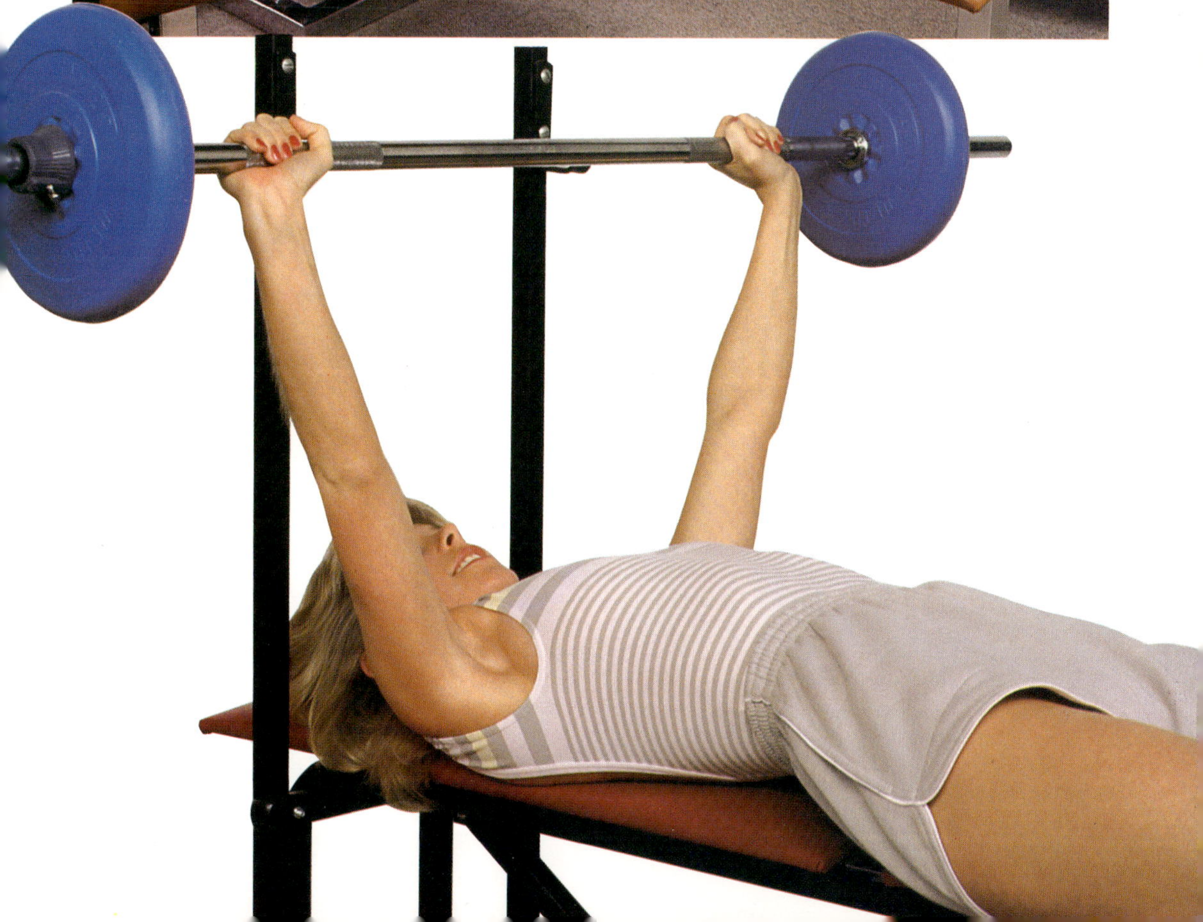

b

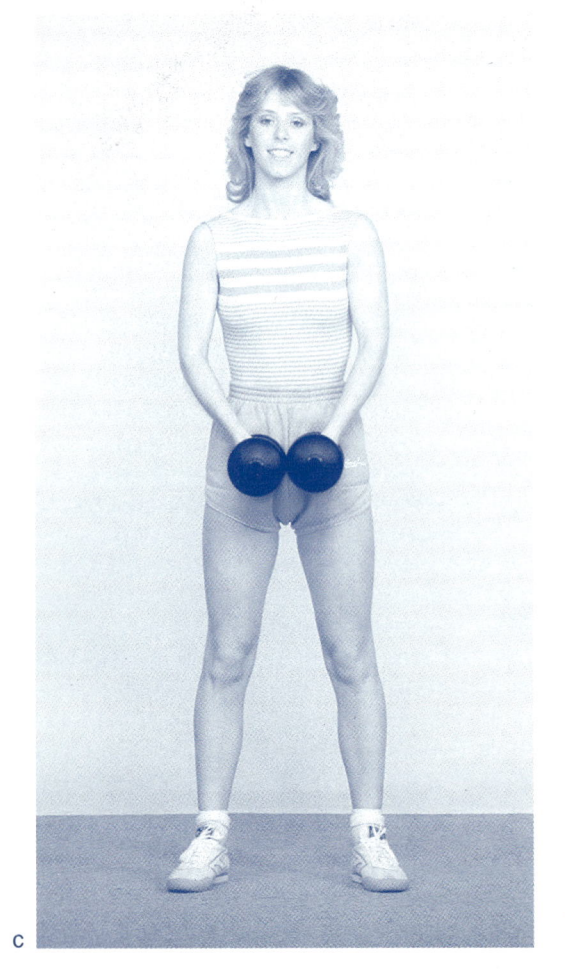

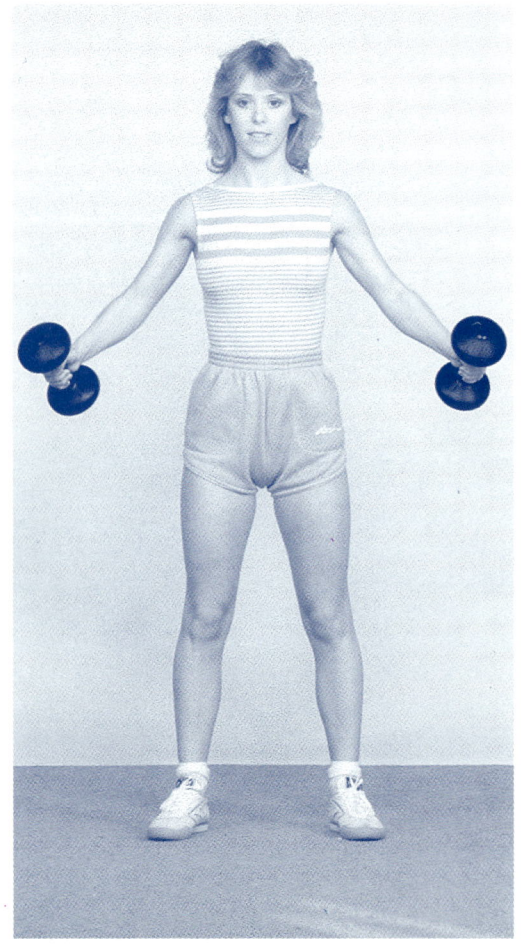

c

b Press behind neck; this is to give a more round shape to bony shoulders. Hold the bar with the hands slightly wider than shoulder width apart.

Start with your arms straight above your head.

Then bring the bar slowly down to the base of the neck, and push back up again. Try to keep your back straight and avoid pushing your chest out too much. Breathe in as you bring the bar down, out as you push back up.

c Dumbell raises. Stand upright with your arms straight down by your sides. Slowly raise the dumbells up until they are above shoulder level, then slowly lower them again. Keep your arms fairly straight but not rigid while doing this.

Breathe in going up, out coming down.

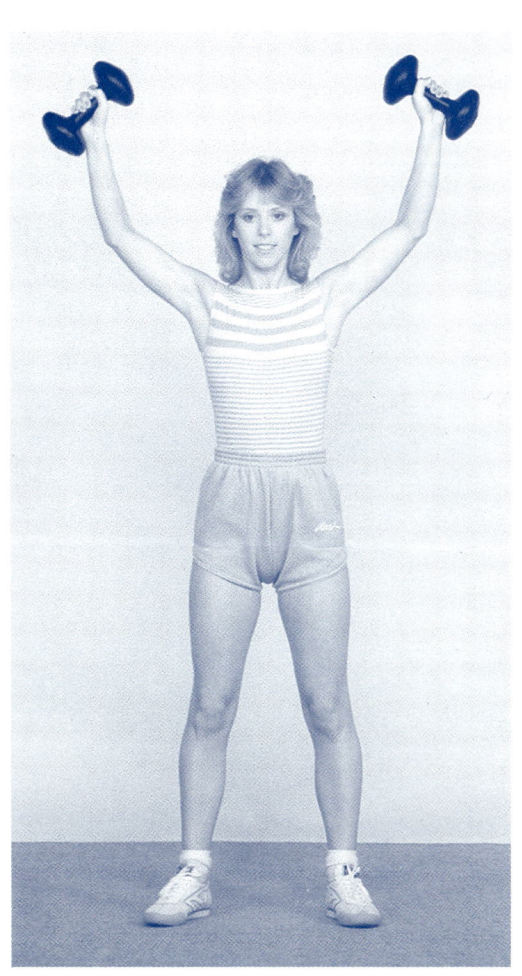

d Flies on the bench. Lying flat on a bench, the starting position is with the arms extended straight, hands together. Pull the knees towards your tummy and cross your ankles (I find this helps to reduce the strain on my back when doing an exercise). Now, bring your arms down to the sides to just below chest level. If your arms are down low, and wide enough, you will be able to feel a stretch across your chest. To help perform the correct movement it may help to imagine a half circle or dome in your mind. Then retrace the movement back to the start position. Breathe in as you bring your arms down, out as you push up.

e Upright rowing. Again this is to help the shoulders and chest, and develop good posture to show your new better shape to advantage. Stand straight, holding the middle of the bar, hands about four or five inches (12 cm) apart. By pushing your elbows out and up, slowly bring your hands up the centre of your body to the base of your neck.

Then slowly lower back down.

Throughout the movement keep your shoulders back and the movement controlled. Do not slump forward at the end.

Breathe in going up, out coming down.

43

Arm Exercises

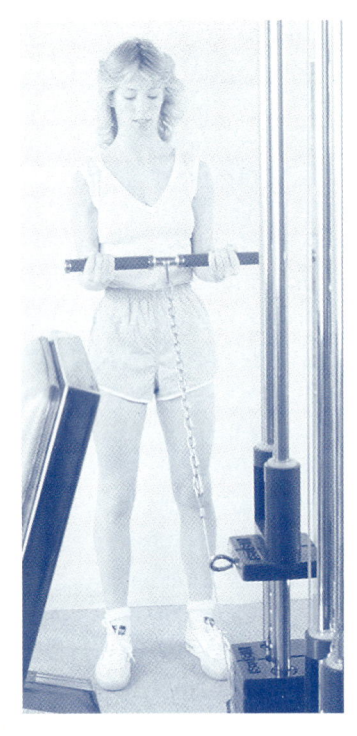

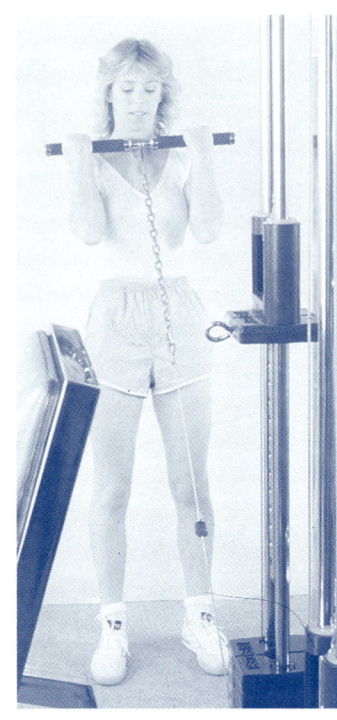

a Biceps curl. The aim of this exercise is not to give you bulging biceps that a man would be proud of, but to firm your arms and improve their shape, so they look fit rather than straight. Hold the bar shoulder width apart, palms upward. Using only the strength in your arms bring the bar up to your shoulders, then lower again. If you are using a weight which is too heavy you will try to help lift it by swinging your back, which is dangerous. Breathe in as you pull up, out as you go down.

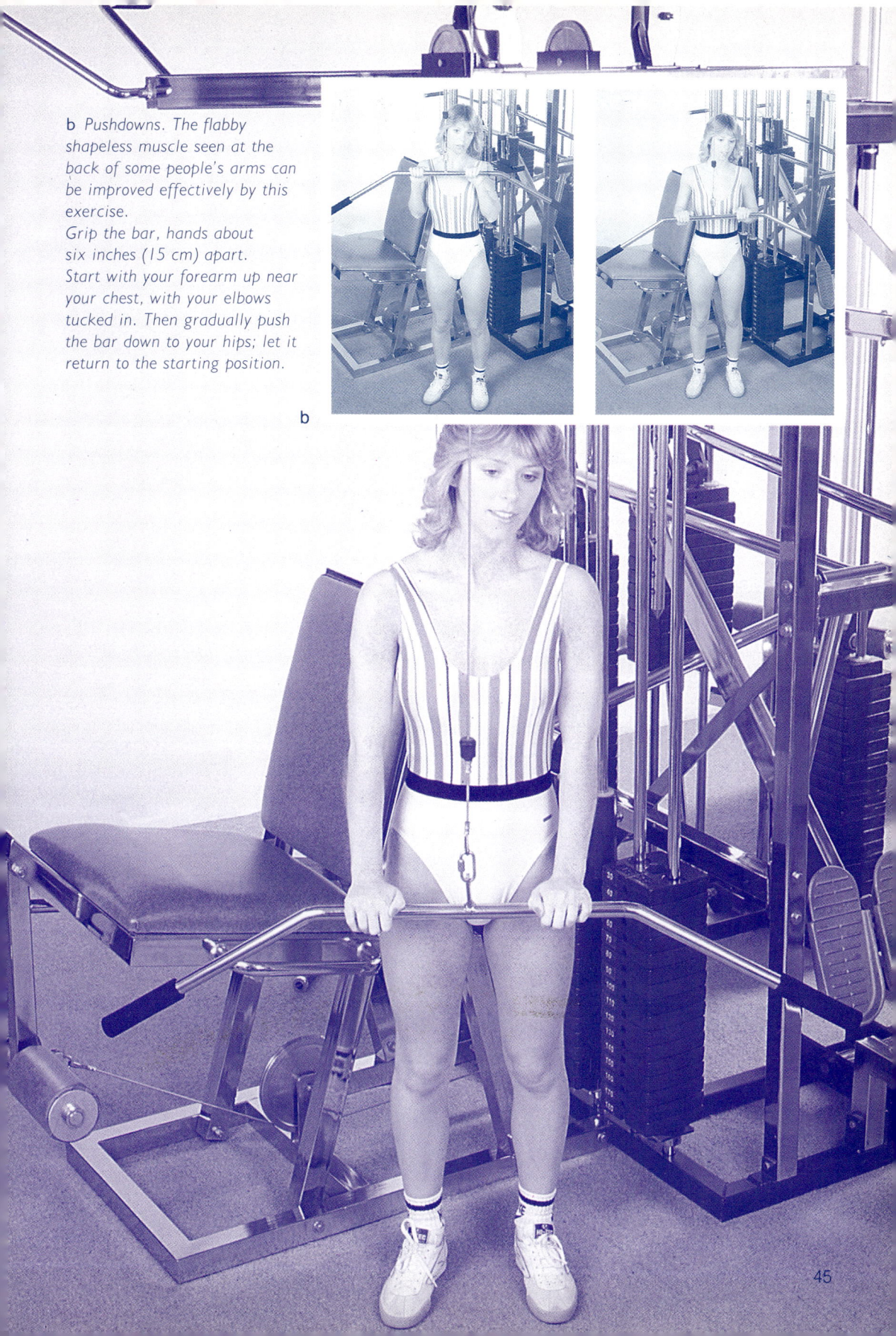

b *Pushdowns.* The flabby shapeless muscle seen at the back of some people's arms can be improved effectively by this exercise.
Grip the bar, hands about six inches (15 cm) apart. Start with your forearm up near your chest, with your elbows tucked in. Then gradually push the bar down to your hips; let it return to the starting position.

b

45

Abdominal and Waist Exercises

a

To get a really flat tummy you need to exercise as well as keeping to a weight-reducing diet. If you are quite a bit overweight, do the leg raises only until you have lost some weight, and then add sit-ups and eventually crunches to your programme.

While doing these exercises, try to hold the abdominal muscles in.

Do as many of these as you can, in three sets (i.e. three times per session).

a Leg raises. Lie on the floor with your hands underneath your sacrum (the bone at the foot of the spine) so that it is slightly lifted off the floor. Slowly raise both legs approximately ten inches (25 cm) from the floor and then lower again, but do not let your feet touch the floor.

b Sit-ups. Lie flat with knees slightly bent, hands behind your head. Pull yourself up into a sitting position, then slowly lower again.

If this is too difficult for you to begin with you may find it easier to put your arms by your sides, palms on the floor, and use your arms to help push yourself up.

Breathe out going up, in coming down.

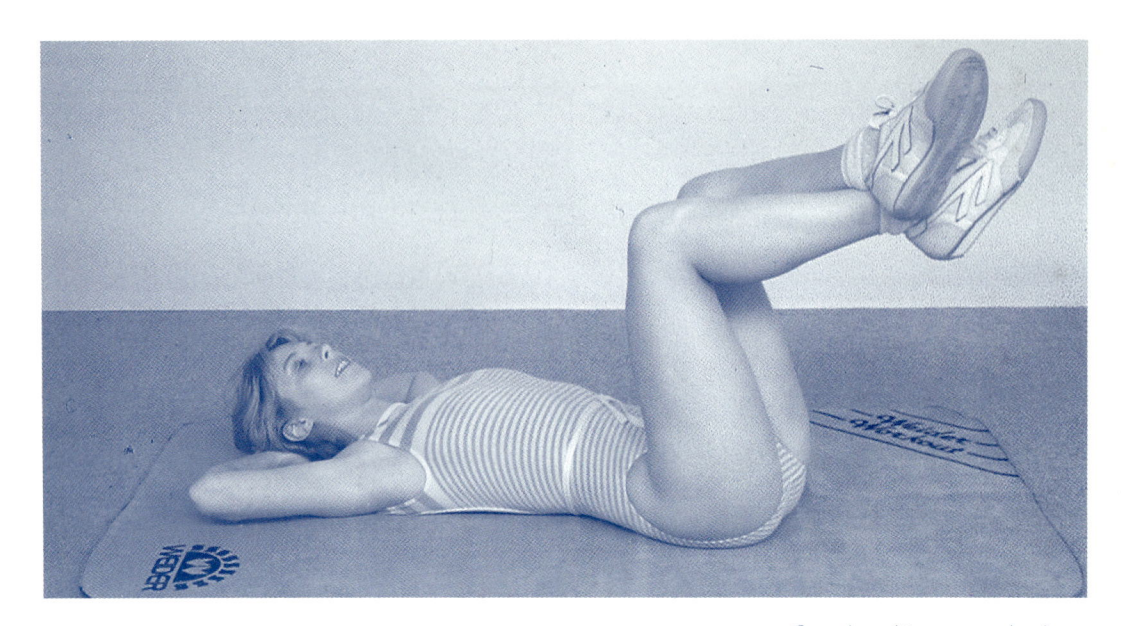

c Crunches. Lie on your back with knees drawn up and ankles crossed. Put your hands behind your head. Pull your shoulders up off the floor, trying to bring your face to your knees, and not your knees to your face.

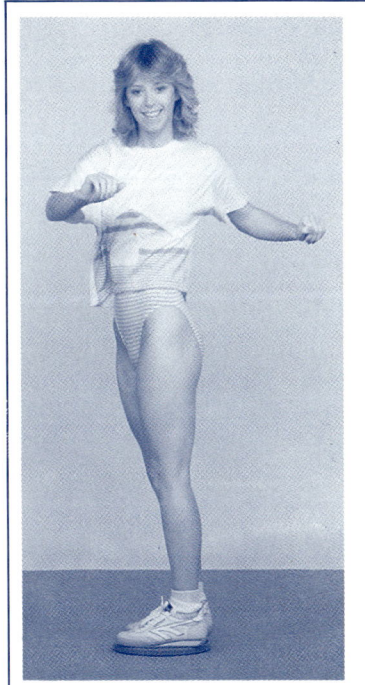

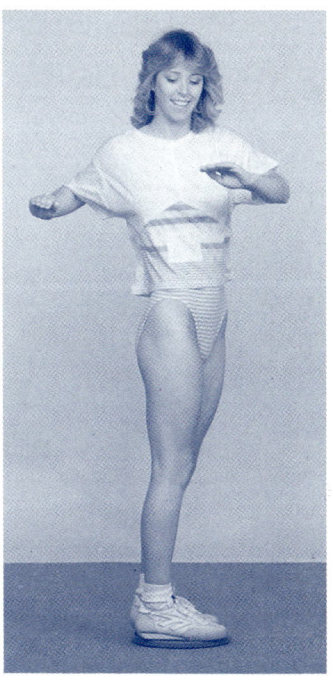

d *Waist twists.* Stand with your feet wider than shoulder width apart. Hold a pole across the back of your neck. Twist only the top half of the body alternately to each side as far as it will go.

It is important that you keep your hips still so that only your waist is twisting. Do as many as you can.

Buttocks Exercises

To firm flabby buttocks, perform the exercises described in the warming-up section: the leg raises lying on your tummy and kick backs from an all-fours position.

Back Exercises

Usually women do not think of their back as being either overweight or underweight, and consequently do not consider exercises for it. However, you will find that if you do some work then your back will develop into a more attractive "V" shape and you will be able to wear strappy tops with more confidence about the view you are presenting from the rear.

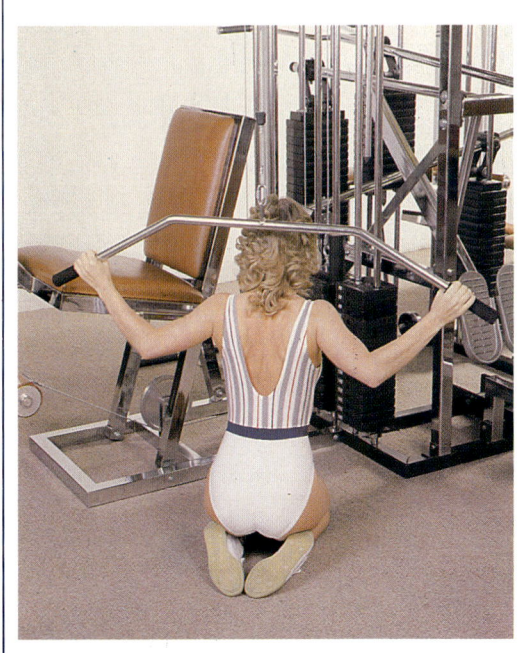

a

Opposite

a Lateral pulldowns. I prefer to do this exercise kneeling on the floor although most people have a stool provided. Hold the bar with a wide grip. Pull the bar down to just past the bottom of your neck, then, slowly, release back up until your arms are stretched as high as they will go. Breathe in as you bring the bar down, out as you stretch up.

b After three sets of this, move your hands closer together and move a little further back from the machine. Repeat the exercise but bringing the bar to the front of the neck and not the back. Moving away from the machine means when you pull the bar down you will be pulling the bar slightly backwards as well as down.

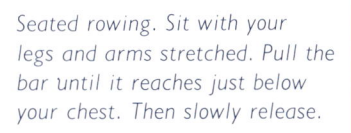

Seated rowing. Sit with your legs and arms stretched. Pull the bar until it reaches just below your chest. Then slowly release.

Avoid the temptation to swing your upper body backwards and forwards or you may damage your back. This exercise in particular is done slowly and deliberately. You may need to use very light weights to avoid swinging your body. Breathe in as you pull the bar to you, out as you release it.

c Bent-over rowing. With your feet wider than shoulder width apart, bend forward, keeping your back straight, with the knees slightly flexed. Hold the bar with the hands shoulder width apart. Bring the bar directly up to your chest and then slowly stretch back down again. Breathe in as you bring the bar up, out as you lower it.

It is most important that you do not jerk your back, or try to lift with your back. Until you are competent at the other exercises you should not do this one.

Winding Down

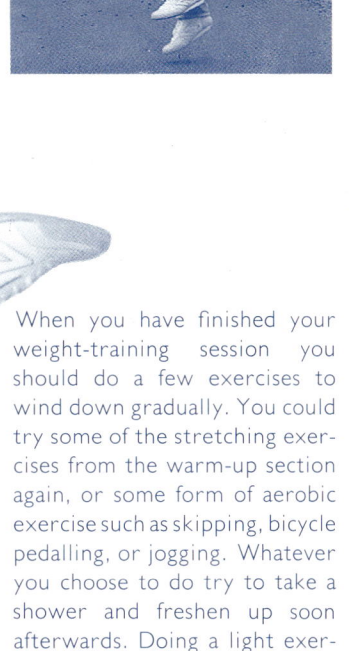

When you have finished your weight-training session you should do a few exercises to wind down gradually. You could try some of the stretching exercises from the warm-up section again, or some form of aerobic exercise such as skipping, bicycle pedalling, or jogging. Whatever you choose to do try to take a shower and freshen up soon afterwards. Doing a light exercise after training helps to prevent that awful stiff feeling that sometimes happens the morning after training.

If you decide to train regularly remember that rest is a vital part of the programme. Do not try to train seven days a week. You will benefit more if you have at least one rest day. Only you can judge the balance between training and rest, so do experiment to see what is best for you.

Equipping a Home Gym

With the provision of readily available purpose-designed equipment it is becoming increasingly popular to have a small gym or at least some facilities at home. There are of course many reasons why some people cannot get to a gym, or prefer to train in the privacy of their own home, away from distractions and the competitive atmosphere of some gyms; and of course you never have to wait for equipment.

The main considerations are space and cost. The room has to be structurally suitable for the type of equipment and the amount of weight you want. For this reason many people choose to use their garage, the car having to take second place. Some form of temporary heating and ventilation may need to be installed. When considering the amount of space available remember that you not only have to consider storage space but the extra space needed to execute some exercises, for example lunges.

There is a comprehensive range of equipment available, ranging from a simple bench to sophisticated equipment seen in commercial gyms. Lots of sports magazines carry advertisements for equipment and it pays to familiarize yourself with what is available before deciding to buy.

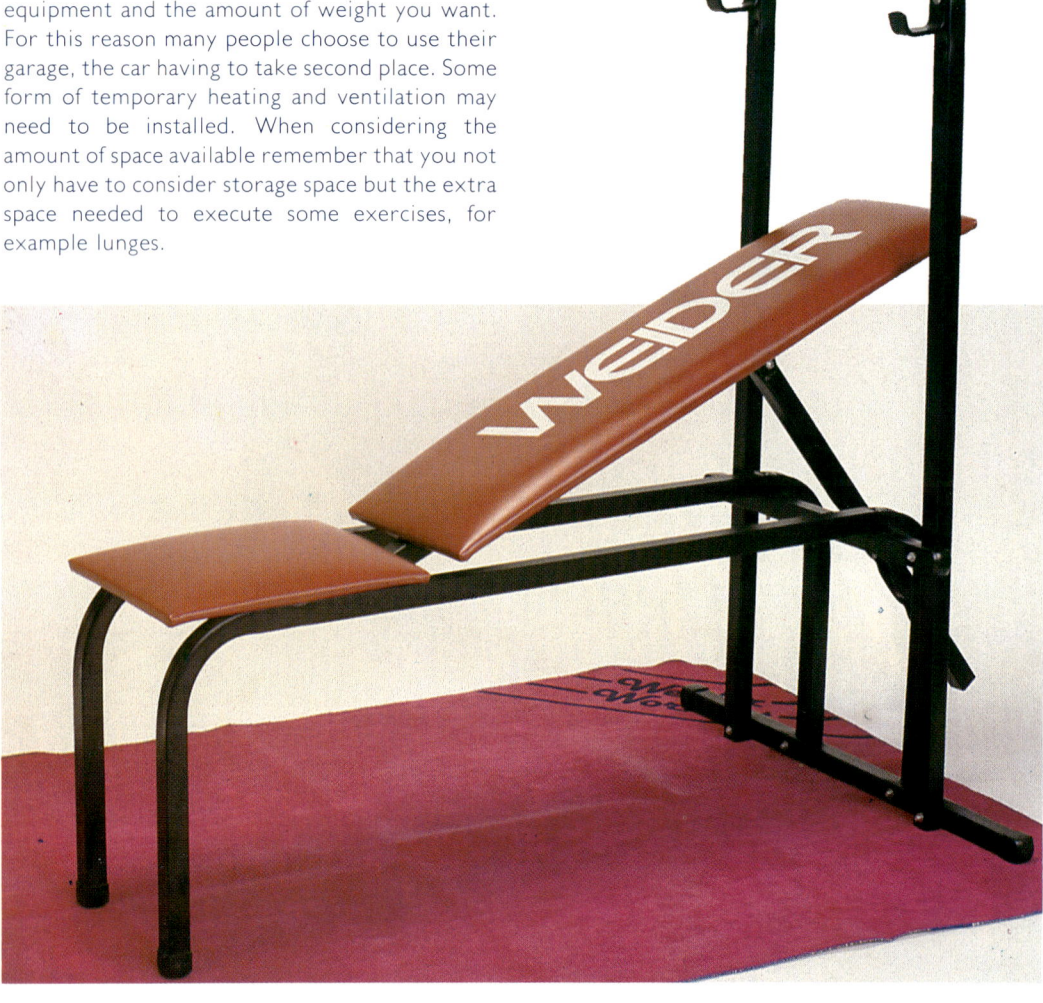

For a basic programme it is possible to manage with a bench and a minimum of equipment. When buying a bench you really need to consider which of its features you actually need, and its sturdiness and durability with regard to the amount of weight you are going to put on it. For example, with most benches you are able to raise the board to an inclined position and alter the height of the stands. Various attachments and extras can be added to extend its range of use.

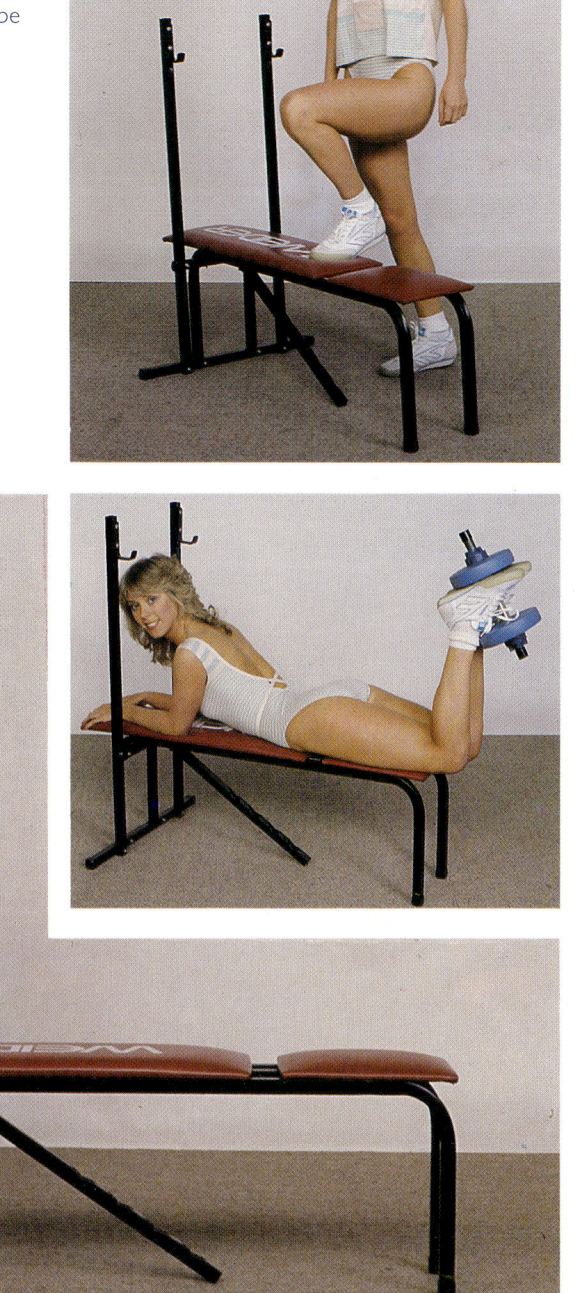

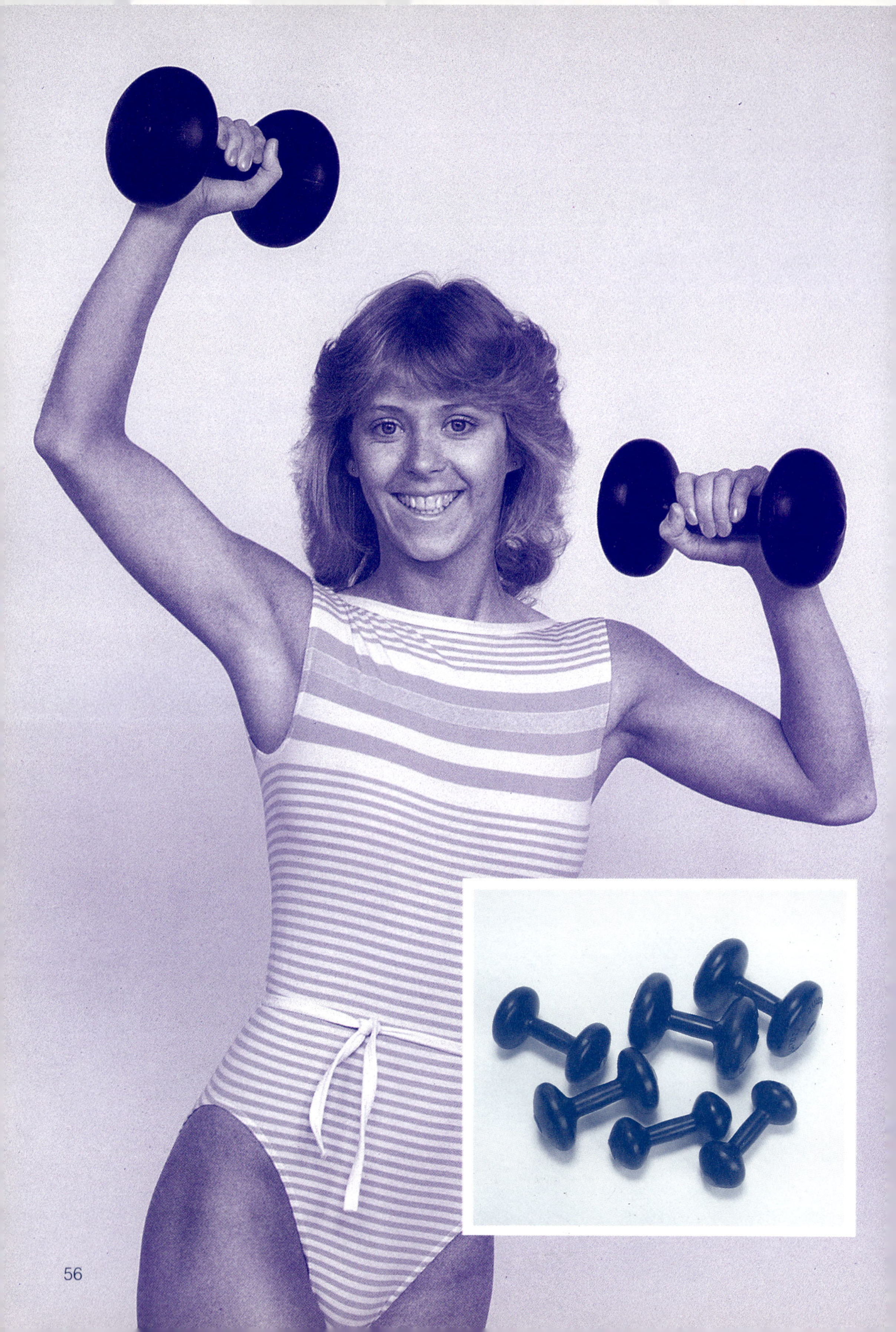

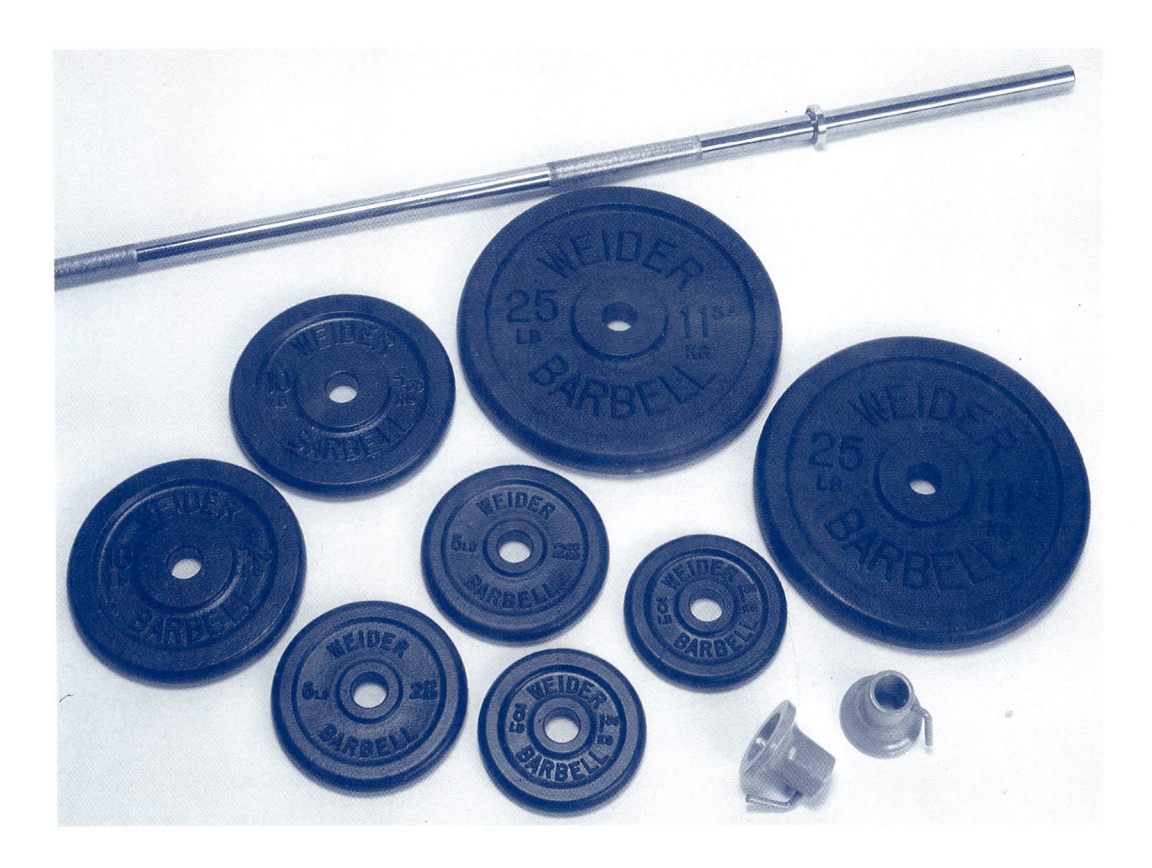

Again, consider what you are actually going to use when buying weights. It is possible to buy either individual weights or a complete set; but do remember your needs will vary according to the exercise you are doing, and of course you will progress. Weights are available that can have extra filling, such as sand, put in them as needed.

For a beginner two weights of 20 lb, two of 10 lb, two of 5 lb and two of 2 lb, with a set of dumbells, should be quite adequate.

You might find a mat useful, as even a carpeted floor is not ideal—it is possible to get carpet burn. To minimize expense, it is possible to be resourceful. Using tins of food as light dumbells is a common example. For a beginner it is satisfactory in several of the exercises to hold a tin in each hand.

Leg curls and thigh extension can be done without purpose-designed equipment if you hold a dumbell between your ankles. Bicycle pedals can be done on the floor lying on your back. Step-ups and calf raises can be done on the stairs. To add extra weight on the calf raises, lean forward so that your arms rest on a step four or five stairs higher than your feet, and then get someone to sit on your flat back.

Equipment need not cost a fortune—a good selection is available by mail order from Weider Health and Fitness, Godalming, Surrey.

If you are thinking of training at home you have to be critical of yourself and aware of mistakes, as obviously there may not be anyone else to point out where you are going wrong, and how to avoid injury. Remember all of the moves you perform should feel natural and within your capabilities. In the exercises I have chosen I have tried to point out where people can go wrong and how to avoid injury. When training on your own you have to be sure that you can lift a weight safely because there may be no one to help you out should you encounter difficulty. As you progress and want to increase the amount of weight used, you will have to increase more gradually by much smaller amounts to avoid the possibility of pinning yourself under a weight you cannot move.

Diet and Vitamins

I am not a dietetics expert and certainly not a good cook, so in this section the aim is to give you some idea of how to use diet to help in your quest for a better body, rather than recommend specific menus and recipes which can be found in many other places. Nowadays many food manufacturers state calorific values of foods on tins or packets. You might also find useful the kind of booklet that gives calorie, fat and carbohydrate contents for a wide variety of foods. Your diet should be an integral part of your fitness programme. Whatever you put into your body will in some way reflect what it looks like from the outside. In this section are included some of the tips and advice I have found useful myself.

Adopting healthy eating habits has to be a gradual process; if you suddenly decide to change your eating habits drastically it is likely to become a short-lived wonder. The best way is gradually to introduce new ideas so that they naturally become part of the diet.

Fresh vegetables and fruit
Fresh vegetables and fruit should be taken daily. The more that is done to vegetables in the way of preparation and cooking the more nutrients will be lost. My habit is to put anything I do not like raw into a pressure cooker which can cook them much faster. If not left in for too long they are still crunchy and full of flavour.

If you do not enjoy plain salads try adding something like apple, rice or pineapple. Experiment to find what you like. Although it reduces the nutritional value I prefer these chopped and mixed together with baked potato. Peeling and boiling potatoes reduces the nutritional value, so they are much better baked in their skins, and of course they have a higher fibre content which greatly improves a healthy diet. I like them with cottage cheese. Cottage cheese is very useful because it is relatively low in fat.

Fats
Most people's diets contain too much fat. You should not aim for a totally fat-free diet as the body needs a balance of fat, protein and carbohydrate. It is the animal sources of fat, such as red meat and dairy foods, that we should try to reduce.

For red meats you can substitute chicken, with the skin removed, or fish. Buy low-fat versions of the dairy produce you cannot resist. If something you want is labelled as "bad for you" then try to find a healthier version first rather than give it up completely, which often leads to cheating later. In foods such as chilli con carne where you would used minced meat, try substituting a soya protein meat—many people cannot tell the difference.

The whole idea of health and fitness is meant to lead to enjoyment, not to be a chore. So if you gradually retrain your taste buds towards natural and healthy food you need not feel you are missing out. The "new" foods will taste so much better than artificial flavourings.

Salt and sugar
I believe that anything made artificially white must be bad for my body. So I try to cut down on the amount of salt I eat, by not adding it to cooking. Vegetables that have not been cooked too much I do not think need extra salt. I also need to keep aware of the amount of salt on crisps, nuts, etc.

Cutting down on sugar is a more difficult problem for me. Where I want to add extra sugar to food, if I cannot resist it then I use honey instead. Breakfast was the biggest problem, but now I enjoy natural yoghurt with bananas, figs, or dried apricots added. If you want to eat tinned rather than fresh fruit then choose a variety tinned in natural juice rather than syrup.

Sweet snack bars and chocolates regularly found their way to my stomach between meals but now I enjoy the more natural versions available from health shops and many supermarkets.

Dieting for weight-loss

The principle of dieting really could not be easier. You just need to use up more energy than you consume in food. Unfortunately in practice it is not easy for many people. There are too many good cooks around! Diets promoted are many and varied but unless one of them can become a regular part of your life-style it is only going to have temporary effects. There are psychological and physiological reasons why crash-diets do not work effectively for any length of time.

If you already eat a healthy diet, then if you eat a little less of it than you did previously, and increase the amount of exercise you take, you should lose weight, and still enjoy it. First of all cut out the snacks in between meals, or substitute a piece of fruit for them. Avoid eating late at night and drink plenty of water to help convince yourself you do not want anything to eat. Regular exercise can increase your metabolism, which is the rate at which your body uses up what you put into it.

If you do cut down drastically on what you eat make sure that you spread out what you do eat over the whole day. Try to make your weight loss gradual so that you adopt a pattern that you can healthily keep to, and you should come to expect less food. The foods to cut out are the ones high in carbohydrate. Numerous guides and charts are available detailing these. You may find that high carbohydrate foods will stimulate your appetite to want more and so set up a vicious circle.

Dieting for weight-gain

The first problem I had when starting weight-training was how to put weight on. I am fortunate enough to have difficulty putting weight on but can appreciate that most people have the reverse problem. I have found it helps me to eat regularly during the day, say at two-hourly intervals, rather than to eat two large meals. I try always to eat healthy foods rather than "junk foods", although I have been known to cheat! It is not always practical or desirable to eat a meal as often as this, so I have supplemented meals with a banana and another piece of fruit, or a snack bar. I have also found that eating at night helps me to put weight on.

Vitamins

Outside of competition training I take one multivitamin tablet a day, although many people tell me that a good balanced diet will provide all of the vitamins and minerals I need. however, I look at it this way: I expect my body to do more in the way of sports and activities than most people do so I prefer to give it extra help, and not leave anything to chance. If you keep to the recommended dose vitamin tablets should do no harm and will provide a back-up system in case the diet is deficient in any vitamin or mineral.

For optimum efficiency, vitamins need to be taken in the correct balance, so unless you know a lot about them it makes sense to take a ready-made preparation. Weider's 'Good Life' multivitamin pack is a well-balanced preparation available from leading health food shops, mail order catalogues, Argos shops or direct from Weider Health and Fitness, Godalming, Surrey.

If I am trying to lose weight and have increased the amount of training I do, and am being more careful about my diet, then I also take Choline and Inositol capsules. They are natural, part of a vitamin complex, and help to utilize fats, but unless diet is controlled and exercise increased there is no reason to take them.

Maintaining Enthusiasm

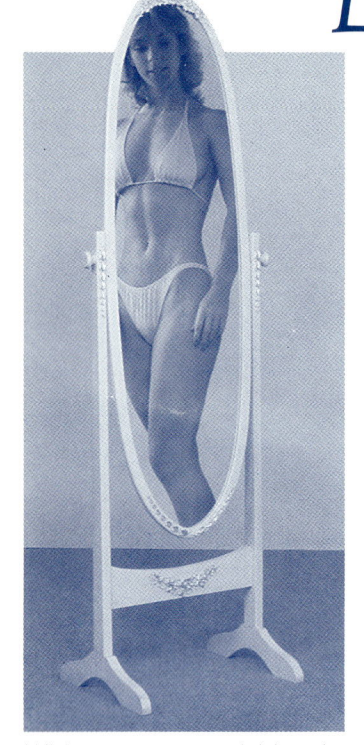

With most new activities the enthusiasm is highest at the beginning, when it is mixed with excitement and hope; and then gradually the novelty starts to wear off. If this happens in your weight training, excuses will start to creep in for missing a session. To get results you have really to keep to your training, working hard regularly.

So, to avoid disappointments, set yourself a target and then begin to monitor your progress. You will be able to satisfy yourself that improvements are coming, and your efforts are being well spent. Weighing yourself is not an accurate way of measuring this progress. It is better to look at yourself in a mirror, with and without clothes, or take measurements, so that you can see your better shape developing. Regularly remind yourself of your improvements. After all, you have to work hard for your success so you deserve to be applauded when you achieve some.

Like most sports, when you first start there is, initially, a rapid improvement in performance and ability, but then, as the the standard rises, improvement slows and seems sometimes hardly apparent. It is at this point that people tend to give up. This is a normal procedure and everyone experiences it, but it can be overcome. If you are in danger of quitting, perhaps it would be a good idea to change something about your programme at this point, with the aim of injecting new life into it and enthusiasm into yourself. You could try changing some of the exercises, trying some new ones, or even altering the order in which you do them. You may find that this rekindles the spark.

All people, if they are honest, will admit to having bad days, days when it really does seem too much effort to go to the gym. Unless these days are frequent and regular it might be best not to go, but do not just sit around doing nothing instead, or you will feel even more disheartened. The most important aspect is to enjoy the training and, if you are not going to do that, it will not hurt to miss a session. I wonder if people train properly in the "forced" session anyway.

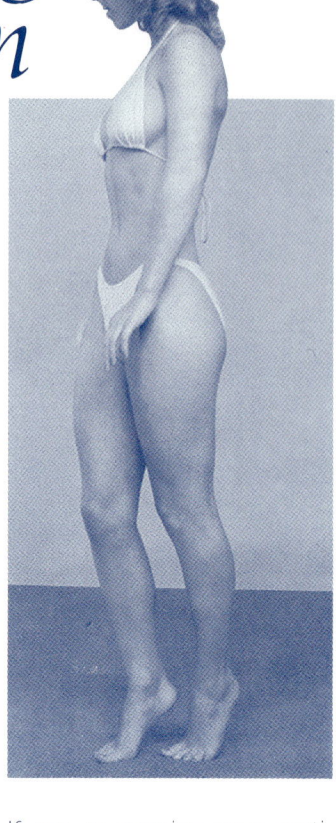

If you re-examine your motivation for training you may find that this fires your enthusiasm again. I find it helpful to look through magazines at photographs and to read about someone else's training.

There may be physical reasons for you not wanting to train, such as tiredness or dysmennorhoea (painful menstruation). Not everyone fits into the same pattern, so you will have to think about your routines and decide if anything can be changed to accommodate a couple of hours in the gym at a time when you *are* feeling energetic. As for the dysmenorrhoea, if you miss out the abdominal exercises you might find that the rest of your training actually helps.

All equipment illustrated in this book was supplied by Weider Health and Fitness, Craven House, Godalming, Surrey. Please write to them for a free catalogue of top-quality equipment and food supplements.